Sharing from the Psalms

Devotions for Women's Groups

Nelle A. Vander Ark

BAKER BOOK HOUSE
Grand Rapids, Michigan 49506

Dedicated to my aunt
ANNA BOUMA DE BOER
who sings praises every day

1. PRAISE FROM SURPRISE

"Bless the Lord, O my soul,
and forget not all his benefits. . . ."
Ps. 103:2a (RSV)

Praise celebrates God. And such celebration cannot be commanded or brought forth simply upon request, such as announcing a song of praise in worship. "Man by creating music, poetry and the like can only *call* for praise. Praise, like joy and love, is one of life's surprises that springs out of the wells of the heart" (Prof. J. Stek).

But what is the source of the spring? What generates the spirit of man so that his mouth and his life overflow with praise? Praise springs from some remembering, some insight, or some discovery of who God is and how He works. We know that God is good and God is great because the Biblical record is clear. But we know it, too, when we see His work in our lives. Such knowing, a combination of remembering and discovering, prompts praise.

When our praise does not flow freely, we ought to consider whether we are giving ourselves the time to remember, to hear, and to discover in truly meaningful ways the works of God. Are we so distracted by "busyness" that we no longer have time to discover the real reasons for praise?

Praise bursts from surprise. Take time to think on God and His ways, "and it will surprise you what the Lord has done." Such surprises will generate not only singing lips and a singing heart but "a *life* made up of praise in every part."

> Sometimes a light surprises
> The Christian while he sings;
> It is the Lord, who rises
> With healing in His wings . . .
>
> In holy contemplation
> We sweetly then pursue
> The theme of God's salvation,
> And find it ever new . . .
> *William Cowper, 1779*

2. PRAISE FOR THE WONDERS OF GOD'S LOVE

"Let them [the redeemed] thank the Lord for his wonderful works to the sons of men."
Refrain from Ps. 107 (RSV)

". . . for his steadfast love endures forever."
Refrain from Ps. 136 (RSV)

Exactly what is it that we are to praise God for? The psalms abound and resound with the answer: the wonders of God's love. In His love God is faithful (steadfast) — always and in all ways. In His love God sought the unlovely and preserved the unloving. In His love God chose Israel and stuck with her in spite of her rebellious spirit. (Check the records the psalmists leave us in Psalms 78, 105, 106, 107, and 136.) When Moses in a fit of impatience with God and with men gave up on God's people, God took up their cause and persisted in loving them to the end. In His love God always does what He says He is going to do!

And the wonder of it all is not just that God worked in this way for Israel and made Himself known then as the only God, whose love and word never fails; but the surprise is that Israel's God is our God today and proved (and goes on proving) the wonders of His unfailing love *in Christ.*

> Joy to the world! The Lord is come.
> Let earth receive her King . . .
>
> He comes to make His blessings flow
> Far as the curse is found . . .
>
> He rules the world with truth and grace,
> And makes the nations prove
> The glories of His righteousness
> And *wonders of His love.*
>
> *Isaac Watts, 1719*

> "Blessed be the Lord, the God of Israel,
> from everlasting to everlasting!
> And let all the people say, 'Amen!'
> Praise the Lord!"
> *Ps. 106:48 (RSV)*

3. PRAISE FOR WINGS

"Oh, that I had wings like a dove. . . ."
Ps. 55:6a (RSV)

Birds are wonderfully free creatures. They rise, they soar, they sing. With their grace of movement and abandonment in song, they have inspired poets and peasants in every land and at all times.

Have you ever wished you were a bird? If you believe God, you are. You have wings. "All God's chillun got wings."

The psalmist wanted to fly away from his troubles and find a comfortable nest for himself. But then God gave him insight to see that in the midst of troubles he could rise even above the birds. He had wings—wings of prayer. "I will call upon God . . . evening, morning, and at noon . . . He will hear me" (Ps. 55:16-17).

And God taught the psalmist that he was a dove—a very special kind of dove. We usually think of a dove in two senses: as a messenger with homing instincts and as an emblem of peace.

The poet Hopkins spoke of man as being "carrier-witted." When man follows such God-given wits (his homing instincts) and uses his wings to fly to God, he soars above his circumstances; he rises far above the doves to heaven itself, singing God's message of peace.

Praise God for wings—wings of prayer, of power, and of peace.

4. PRAISE FOR BELONGING

"Happy the people whose God is the Lord!"
Ps. 144:15b (RSV)

"O God, thou art my God ...
my lips will praise thee."
Ps. 63:1a, 3b (RSV)

Praise God we are human—that is, we were created to belong—to belong to God. But because we are fallen in our humanness, we resist God. Self and pride must first be washed away by the blood and spirit of the self-denying Savior.

Then, after being renewed, because we are human—created to belong—we love to feel God's arms around us. The arm of conquest becomes the arm of comfort, and the *grip of possession is the clasp of friendship.*

And we are happy in the service of our Master, happy to be what God intended us to be: human—dependent, but free. We are creatures filled with the power and the life of our Creator—power to think, to imagine, to produce, to rule, to love, and to enjoy (Ps. 8:5-8).

When God looked on His finished creation, He said, "It is very good." And now recreated man echoes the song: "How good it is to be alive—alive unto God—to be a person, a human being, with real purpose for living and God's power to express it."

> Ye people who worship Jehovah,
> His praises with gladness proclaim;
> His servants, and all ye that fear Him,
> Sing praise to His glorious name.
>
> O Church of our God, sing His praises,
> *For with you and in you He dwells;*
> O sing hallelujahs before Him,
> Whose glory all praises excels.
> *Ps. 135 (metrical version)*

5. PRAISE ON MONDAY MORNING

"Cast your burden on the Lord, and he will sustain you;
he will never permit the righteous to be moved."

Ps. 55:22 (RSV)

"Casting all your care upon him; for he careth for you."

I Peter 5:7 (KJV)

One of my choicest early childhood memories is that of hearing my mother sing. She was not a great singer as we speak of singers today, but she had a great capacity for song—a singing heart and a storehouse of memorized songs. My most vivid memory of her singing is the song she so often sang on Monday morning while she was busy doing the laundry for our large family. She sang so clearly and so cheerily:

> How sweet, my Savior, to repose
> On thine almighty power!
> To feel thy strength upholding me
> Through every trying hour!
>
> Casting all your care upon Him,
> Casting all your care upon Him,
> Casting all your care upon Him
> For He careth, He careth for you.
>
> *Caesar Malan*

Oh, my mother knew the secret of praise—trust in God. "In God, whose word I praise, in God I trust without a fear" (Ps. 56:10, RSV). That trust gave her a song even on Monday mornings.

The God who gave her such trust and songs of praise is the same God we confess. He is still working in our lives and in the world today. Praise Him! Sing to Him every day.

> How good it is to thank the Lord,
> And praise to thee, Most High, accord,
> To show thy love with morning light,
> And tell thy faithfulness each night;
> Yea, good it is thy praise to sing,
> And all our sweetest music bring.
>
> *Ps. 92 (metrical version)*

6. PRAISE FOR RENEWAL

*"Restore to me the joy of thy salvation . . .
and my tongue will sing aloud of thy deliverance."*
Ps. 51:12a, 14b (RSV)

In the mercy of God a broken "connection" between us and God can be made "live" again. There is only one way, however, to such renewal — unqualified, complete *confession*. To experience the joy of forgiveness and the renewal of our total being (the two most indispensable elements for praise) we need to come to God and say, *"I was wrong. I was dead wrong. O God, in Your mercy make me right again."*

That was David's prayer in Psalm 51. Following his confession and plea for mercy, he experienced having all the old dirt scrubbed out of his life and felt a new white cleanness entering in. His bad record was erased, and he was given a chance to live again as if nothing had ever happened.

But David knew, in a way that he had never known before, how much he needed God to take over, control, and empower every single part of his being so that he might stay clean and live right — every day in every way. When David came to that point, he found God's gracious renewal in all of his life. He experienced renewal of *mind* — a better understanding of sin and a better sense of truth (v. 6). His *heart* and his *will* were renewed. He prayed to have the craving for sin taken away and to have instead a spirit that craved for God (v. 10). And finally, he had a renewed *testimony*. Because he knew how much he had been forgiven, he had something to sing about (v. 14b).

With the stain and the strain of sin removed, David could say with unrestrained grace: "O Lord, open thou my lips, and my mouth shall show forth thy praise" (v. 15).

7. PRAISE FOR USEFULNESS

"Restore to me the joy of thy salvation,
and uphold me with a willing spirit.
Then will I teach transgressors thy ways,
and sinners will return to thee."

Ps. 51:12-13 (RSV)

Everyone wants to be useful. But not everyone enjoys David's insight for the way to usefulness.

We all know that the useful life is the life that has a sense of obligation—we "have promises to keep." What gives us this sense of "oughtness," this sense of wanting and needing to give something of ourselves to another? We learn from David's experience as related in Psalm 51 that a full consciousness of forgiveness gives us a sense of obligation and a real motive for service. When we realize the great debt that God has paid for us, we want to do something for Him to show how much we appreciate what He did. In this way a sense of service is born.

When we know something of our sinfulness and have experienced God's forgiving love and renewing power, we want to share the good news with others—help them find the way to life and joy. Could it be that our witness often lacks verve because we lack a real consciousness of cleansing and thus have no real joy of salvation to share?

Read again David's words at the beginning of this meditation. His determination to *teach others the ways of God* will give you a renewed sense of usefulness. You will sense anew that you're on earth to carry out God's business. Praise God for the privilege, and sing with an understanding heart and renewed spirit:

I'm here on business for my King!
This is the message that I bring,
A message angels fain would sing,
'O be ye reconciled,' thus saith my Lord and King;
'O be ye reconciled to God!'

8. PRAISE FOR THE WORD

*"Take the veil from my eyes, that I may see the
marvels that spring from thy law."*
                                    Ps. 119:18 (NEB)

I recall walking with a child on a rainy day. As we
hurried from one place of shelter to the next, she said,
"I don't like rain. It gets in the way of my eyes."

Daily there are things that "get in the way of our
eyes," things that dim our view or blur our vision.
There are times when we stand in our own light, when
we are so preoccupied with "feeling good about ourselves" or seeking the approval of others that we cannot see God and have no real desire to walk God's way.

When God removes the veil of earthly things or
selfish ambitions from our eyes, then we can see the
wonders of God's love and of His directions (law) for
our lives. We "see the light" and experience the delight
of "seeing straight." We see God anew and receive a
renewed desire to please Him more than anything else.

Praise God for unveiling our eyes and revealing the
path of life. Praise for the Word!

SONG:

Open my eyes that I may see
Glimpses of truth thou hast for me.

9. PRAISE FOR SINGLE-MINDEDNESS

"Blessed are those . . . who seek him with their whole heart."

Ps. 119:2 (RSV)

"I hate men who are not single-minded, but I love thy law."

Ps. 119:113 (NEB)

Give me the single eye
Thy name to glorify

Ps. 86 (metrical version)

We sing, "Consecrate me now to thy service, Lord, by the power of grace divine." We sing it easily, but it's desperately hard to live a consistently consecrated life. Consecration requires concentration—study of what God says really counts in life.

We live in a world of distractions, activities cluttering up our minds and lives so that we hardly know what to do first. We are so busy, sometimes even with things that seem so worthy, that we scarcely have time to think.

Oh, for more of the delightful single-mindedness that the psalmist sought. Lord, help us to get rid of the excess baggage in our lives, to "travel light." Give us the wisdom to say no to any invitation that would interfere with our being close to You. Give us the power of concentration so that we may praise You as we ought with a lively singleness of heart.

PRAYER:

Eternal Spirit, God of truth,
Our contrite hearts inspire;
Kindle a flame of heavenly love,
And feed the pure desire.

Subdue the power of every sin,
Whate'er that sin may be,
That we, *in singleness of heart*,
May worship only Thee.

T. Cotterill, 1810

10. PRAISE FOR POSITION

"I am thy servant; give me insight to
understand thy instruction."
Ps. 119:125 (NEB)

There is an old song that often runs through my mind:

Only an armor-bearer, proudly I stand,
Waiting to follow at the King's command,
Marching if "Onward" should the order be,
Standing by my Captain, serving faithfully.

The psalmist understood well such a position. He knew his place and was happy in it.

Servanthood is not slavery. It's status. It begins with an attitude of heart and mind whereby one gladly yields to God the right-of-way in his life. Then it becomes a position of readiness and responsibility. And it continues as a school where one has the opportunity to learn from his favorite teacher.

A faithful, obedient servant, happy in His service, is a tribute to Christ, who gave His life in service and, in so doing, taught us the beauty and the price of being God's servant.

PRAYER:
Here I am, Lord, at Your service today. Help me to understand Your orders and to carry them out just as You'd like.

A THOUGHT FOR THE DAY:
An ancient Roman coin is inscribed with a picture of an ox facing an altar and a plow, and the words: Ready for either. This is the formula of faith.

11. PRAISE IN RIVERS OF SONG

"I will praise the name of God with a song. . . ."
                                    Ps. 69:30a (ASV)

"Jehovah is my strength and my shield;
 My heart hath trusted in him, and I am helped;
 Therefore my heart greatly rejoiceth;
 And with my song will I praise him."
                                    Ps. 28:7 (ASV)

I have just spent a delightful half hour with the Bible and a hymn book. I think I know a bit more of what it's like to pour out your praises in rivers of song. Just noting again some of the many references to song in the Book of Psalms and the invitations (commands?) to "sing praises" made me feel as if I could fill a book about singing. I sang one song after another and saw anew the genius of the psalms—they *sing* their way into one's being and they flood the soul with rivers of song.

How are we going to store up these waters so that from our hearts and mouths will flow steady streams of praise in song? One obvious, but often neglected, way is to *memorize* good songs, songs that are filled with the truth and beauty of Scripture. Build a storehouse of song—in yourself and in others. (One of my favorite gifts to new parents is a hymn book for children.) And then, keep the material fresh in your memory by much practice. Sing in the morning; sing at night. "It is a good thing . . . to sing praises . . . in the morning . . . every night" (Ps. 92:1-2, ASV).

Sing joyfully—exultingly! Keep singing lest you cease praising!

Now with joyful exultation let us sing Jehovah's praise
To the Rock of our salvation loud hosannas let us raise. . . .
                                    Ps. 95 (metrical version)

12. PRAISE FOR THE SEA

"The sea is his, for he made it . . ."
Ps. 95:5a (RSV)

"He rebuked the Red Sea, and it became dry . . ."
Ps. 106:9a (RSV)

Some Christians today are beginning to question the truth of the old song:

> This is my Father's world
> O let me ne'er forget
> That though the wrong seems oft so strong
> God is the Ruler yet!

May we still sing it? Of course! We ought to sing it more confidently than ever. The God who made the sea and rebuked the sea *owns* the sea. And He has not abdicated His position nor relinquished one bit of His power. The forces of evil are strong, the work of Satan is frightening, his existence is real, but the Creator and Redeemer of the world rules the world. Satan and all his hosts can go no farther than God allows them to go. Pharaoh, the instrument of Satan, pursued Israel, the people of God, into the sea. "But the sea overwhelmed their enemies [Pharaoh's hosts]. And He [God] brought them [Israel] to his holy land." (Ps. 78:53b-54a, RSV). And the God of the Red Sea and of all Pharaohs is our God (Ps. 95:7).

SONG:

> In His hand are earth's deep places,
> His the strength of all the hills,
> His the sea whose bounds He traces,
> His the land His bounty fills.
> *Ps. 95 (metrical version)*

13. PRAISE FOR PERSON

"I praise Thee because I have been
fearfully and wonderfully made;
marvelous is Thy workmanship,
as my soul is well aware."
Ps. 139:14 (NBV)

Modern society is obsessed with the need for a healthy "self-concept." Education and training at all levels and in all areas is geared toward making each person "feel good about himself."

Praise for self, for one's personhood, is Biblical. The catch, however, is that the praise is not in and for the person but in and to the God who made and remade the person. The psalmist sets the pattern for us: "I praise Thee because I have been . . . wonderfully made; . . . *Thy workmanship."*

When we see the subtle distinction between praising self and praising God for self, we have reached a new level of self-concept and will steadily find more reasons for praise. When we acknowledge that the source of our being, the root of our existence, is in God and in Him alone, we have inexhaustible resources for living—for "feeling good"—today and always.

Then we sing with fresh insight and revived, steady energy:

All that I am I owe to thee;
Thy wisdom, Lord, has fashioned me,
I give my Maker thankful praise,
Whose wondrous works my soul amaze.

Ere into being I was brought,
Thine eye did see, and in thy thought
My life in all its perfect plan
Was ordered ere my days began.
Ps. 139 (metrical version)

14. PRAISE FOR THE SEARCHING EYE

"Thou hast searched me, Lord,
and Thou knowest me . . .
Thou hast closed me in behind and in front,
and hast placed Thy hand upon me."

Ps. 139:1, 5 (NBV)

Why is it that Psalm 139 often evokes more fear than praise? The choice of words indicates that God is very close to man: God *searches, knows, surrounds,* and *touches* man. Such closeness can be very uncomfortable, but the psalmist rejoices in it. What makes the difference? The writer of this psalm not only stands in awe of God but he has also learned to trust God.

When trust is established, the searching eye is like an x-ray used by a loving doctor to detect anything that might possibly be wrong so that it can be eradicated. The surrounding arm of God is the embrace of a loving Father. The touching hand is the clasp of a Friend "who sticks closer than a brother."

And the marvel of it all is, says the psalmist, that such a big, awesome God knows and loves not only *all* His works but also little *me* and takes my hand every day to keep me on the path of life.

PRAYER:

Search me, O God, and know my heart,
Try me, my thoughts to know;
O lead me, if in sin I stray
In paths of life to go.

Ps. 139 (metrical version)

15. PRAISE FOR PURPOSE

"Thou dost show me the path of life. . . ."
Ps. 16:11a (RSV)

Some of the most tragic lines ever written are found in Robert Frost's poem "The Death of the Hired Man." Silas, the hired man, had never been able to find his place in life. Homeless and helpless, he came back to one of his farmer-employers, hoping to find one last bit of comfort before he died. The wife of the farmer pleaded with her husband to take Silas in, and in portraying his plight, she said:

> Poor Silas! nothing to look back upon with pride
> And nothing to look forward to with hope.

What worthlessness and despair Silas must have suffered!

Without God every one of us is a Silas, a helpless, hopeless case. With God, with His grace beaming into our lives and lighting each step of life for us, we have worth — and purpose.

We have everything to live for and something to die for. God gives purpose. God gives life! Praise Him!

> What about the man who trusts in God
>   and is committed to His purposes?
> He is a man who is rich indeed . . .
> He is a man with purpose and meaning in his life.
> He is the man through whom God is
>   working out His purposes in this world today.
> *(Selected lines from an anonymous*
> *paraphrase of Psalm 112)*

16. PRAISE FOR HOME

*"O Lord, Thou hast been our home
in successive generations."*
                    Ps. 90:1 (NBV)

Where do you live? Do you live alone? Common
questions to which children of God can give uncommon
answers: "God is my home. So, really, I am always at
home, and I am never alone." True, our feelings don't
always fall in line with these facts, but the facts stand.

What tranquility we can enjoy every day quietly
and steadily living with God and knowing that God
has come to live with us—not as a weekend guest but
as a permanent resident, an ever-gracious, providing
Host and a never-failing Friend.

Is there anything at all required of us? Yes. To live
with God we must stay home and gladly obey the rules
of the household. And, contrary to all popular notions,
the kind of staying home required of God's family is
not boring or confining. Life with God is adventurous
and free.

The psalmist found such life so desirable that he was
willing to drop everything else and pursue only that
"one thing."

> "One thing I ask of the Lord,
> One thing I seek:
> That I may be constant in the house of the Lord
> All the days of my life."
>
> *Ps. 27:4a (NEB)*

If such a resolute desire is ours, we may claim all
the comforts of God's home now and sing praises
eternally:

> "Surely goodness and mercy shall follow me
>   all the days of my life
> And I shall dwell in the house of the Lord forever."
>
> *Ps. 23:6 (RSV)*

17. PRAISE FOR DELIVERANCE FROM DECEPTION

"Blessed is the man . . . in whose spirit there is no deceit."
Ps. 32:2 (RSV)

In the dead of night a weasel once entered my brothers' rabbit coops. It slipped in and out again without the slightest noise or disturbance. No one saw it come; no one saw it go. But we knew that it had been there, for in the morning there was the evidence of its attack— all the rabbits lay dead, a tiny hole in their necks where their blood had been drained from them. It was a sickening sight. It was hard even for boys with brave hearts to keep back the tears as they picked up their lifeless pets, put them into a tub, and buried them out in the field!

There is a weasel-like thing at work in everyone's soul. It works so quietly that it is difficult to detect and to expose. But it is there, and unless we recognize its real character, it will sap our life-blood too. It is the thing that talks to us something like this: "You have a mind of your own. Don't let anybody run your life. You have a right to be whatever you would like to be." Or, sometimes this weasel-like thing is so subtle that we can't exactly state just what it tells us, but we know it is at work. If we really stop to think about the why of many of our actions—even those that seem so noble— we can see the big I or the proud self in us, slithering around and constantly maneuvering for its own advantage.

Are you aware of this selfish, conniving rascal at work in your heart? If you are not, pray hard for God to open your eyes before your life and all your ambitions fall into a worthless heap, like the pile of dead rabbits killed by the weasel. But if you know a little bit about how selfish and proud you are and are fighting it daily, there is real comfort for you. The struggle with self is a sign that God is working in your heart. Just give yourself over to God and praise Him for delivering you from deceiving yourself.

18. PRAISE FOR THE GUIDING EYE

"I will instruct thee and teach thee
in the way which thou shalt go:
I will guide thee with mine eye."
Ps. 32:8 (KJV)

A planning committee was discussing proposals for the next year's activities. As various suggestions were made, one member quietly listened but steadily looked at the teacher-leader. She watched for the eye of approval or disapproval. At one point she noted a troubled look, an uneasy expression, in the eyes of the instructor. At that point that sensitive committee member questioned the proposed action by saying, "I see the raised eyebrow in our teacher and would like to know her feelings on this matter." There was an instance of eye-contact and guidance with an eye.

The text above appears in a well-known psalm of confession. From confession arises praise for forgiveness and promise for future direction so that slipping into sin again may be avoided. The eye of the Lord is upon us not only to keep us but also to teach us, to guide us into life—life on a higher plane. For such living we have but to look at God's face steadily as He unveils (reveals) it for us in the Word (both in the Bible and in Christ) and watch His eyes for approval or disapproval. In so doing, we will learn to "read Him like a book."

Follow His guiding eye. Know when He frowns; know also when He smiles. Then lift your heart in praise for His loving direction:

I graciously will teach thee
The way that thou shalt go,
And with Mine eye upon thee
My counsel make thee know.
Ps. 32 (metrical version)

19. PRAISE FOR A PLACE TO HIDE

"Thou art a hiding place for me,
thou preservest me from trouble;
thou dost encompass me with [shouts of] deliverance."
Ps. 32:7 (RSV)

Every time I cross the vast plains of the Dakotas, I think of the woman in the novel *Giants in the Earth* who almost lost her mind in this treeless land because there was "no place to hide." She needed the solace found only in solitude and some feeling of support to face all the stress around her and within her. Because there was "no place to hide," she found no such relief and thus became ever more distressed.

The psalms reveal many different ways in which God is a refuge and tell about the many provisions He makes for us when we are in hiding — hiding in God. A rather strange twist is that God provides us with protection from Himself. It is clear from Psalm 32 that, when we confess our sins, God provides a covering for them so that they are hidden from His sight. We are sheltered from His anger and saved from His punishment.

As we continue to hide in God and His word (Ps. 119:114), we find security in all circumstances and supplies for all our needs. There is protection from all that would wound us, a shield to ward off the "fiery darts" of temptation, and a resting-place for steady refreshment and refueling.

Hiding in God is not seeking escape from the world. It is experiencing the fullness of salvation and then learning from God how to face the world and to redeem it. As we stay with God and let Him be our only hiding place, we can enjoy the exuberant faith of the psalmist:

> "The Lord is my light and my salvation;
>   whom shall I fear?
> The Lord is the stronghold [refuge] of my life;
>   of whom shall I be afraid?"
> Ps. 27:1-2 (RSV)

20. PRAISE FOR SOLITUDE

"For God alone my soul waits in silence. . . ."
Ps. 62:1a, 5a (RSV)

"Be still, and know that I am God."
Ps. 46:10 (RSV)

Many of us are engaged in work that takes us away from home for periods of time. Such travel is often exciting but sometimes tiring. We speak of being "travel-worn" or experiencing jet-lag. We feel the need for refueling.

The psalmist, too, had many unsettling, wearying experiences—enemies steadily threatening his God-given kingship and liars taunting his commitment to God and His ways. Time and again David speaks of his need for rest and renewal of strength and hope. For such times when he needed to "get it all together" again, he, like Christ, sought quietude. By spending time with God, in solitude and silence, he received renewed energy, vision, and confidence for the next assignment.

The need for such solitude is emphasized throughout Scripture. It is not the same as loneliness, a distraught state of mind when one feels deserted by God and man. It is rather a peaceful disposition of the soul when one feels close to God and confident that God is and will always be his foundation ("rock"), his salvation (healing), his shelter, his "strength for today and bright hope for tomorrow."

Power comes from being quiet with God. "In quietness and in trust shall be your strength" (Isa. 30:15b, RSV). Read all of Psalm 62 quietly, "pour out your heart before him" (v. 8a) as you read; and in the end, alone with God, joyfully join the psalmist in his words of praise: ". . . power belongs to God and to thee, O Lord, belongs steadfast love" (v. 11b-12a).

21. PRAISE IN THE CONGREGATION

"Praise the Lord.
I will give thanks to the Lord with my whole heart,
in the company of the upright, in the congregation."
                              Ps. 111:1 (RSV)

"I will tell of thy name to my brethren;
in the midst of the congregation I will praise thee."
                              Ps. 22:22 (RSV)

"I have told the glad news of deliverance
in the great congregation. . . ."
                              Ps. 40:9a (RSV)

To have a time and a place to meet with God privately is a necessary first step for a life of praise. (See Christ's words on private prayer in Matt. 6:6.) But those who experience God's mercy and are filled with His power in private will give expression to it in public. Such expression uplifts both the speaker and the hearers and pleases God no end.

How will such expressions be made? The psalmist says repeatedly there will be open, spontaneous testimonies "in the congregation." There will be freedom to speak in God's house of "what he [God] has done for me" (Ps. 66:13-16). There will be times in the worship services for people to share their gratitude with others (Ps. 22:22). There will be much music and communication in song. When Paul commanded Spirit-filled people to "speak to one another in psalms, hymns, and spiritual songs" (Eph. 5:19, ASV), he was re-echoing the spirit of the psalmist and prescribing a way for the church of all ages to express its praise.

The Word of the Lord is clear: public expressions of praise are obligatory, not optional.

God, help us to praise You freely, joyously, glorifyingly "in the congregation."

> Amid the thronging worshipers
> Jehovah will I bless;
> Before my brethren, gathered there,
> His name will I confess.
>   *Ps. 22 (metrical version)*

22. PRAISE FOR TRIAL

*"How good it is for me to have been punished,
to school me in thy statutes."*

Ps. 119:71 (NEB)

*"O how I love thy law . . . for thou thyself
hast been my teacher."*

Ps. 119:97a, 102b (NEB)

Suffering, like schooling, can be grinding. Grinding can wear something thin, or it can sharpen and polish. The grinding of affliction in God's school is God's way to produce "refined" people.

One of the grandest expressions in literature is the opening line of "The Wreck of the Deutschland", a poem by G.M. Hopkins. The *Deutschland* was a German ship sailing to England in the mid 1800s. On board were five godly nuns, exiled from Germany and seeking refuge in England. They were nearing harbor when the ship was wrecked in the English Channel. All on board were drowned. The poet wrestled with the ways of God in allowing such a catastrophe. Through the straining struggle he gained a new perspective: what was to man a shipwreck was to God a harvest. And he rose to new heights of praise. His poetic account of it all begins with this striking exclamation: "Thou mastering me God!" And the poet delighted in such mastery, like David and all who have been through another course in God's school of suffering. Hopkins discovered anew that by being conquered by the Lord who made him and remade him, he gained the freedom to be what God intended him to be.

O Thou mastering me God, how I love thy mastery! What a confession! Do we dare to say it? We're asking for trouble if we do, but trouble schools us in God's ways and teaches us the wonders of His grace.

O Thou mastering me God, how I love Thy law — also the law of Thy kingdom that by suffering I am blessed and by being mastered I am free!

My God, how wonder-full Thou art!

23. PRAISE FOR PEACE

"Great peace have those who love thy law;
nothing can make them stumble."
                              Ps. 119:165 (RSV)

"Peace be unto you all that are in Christ."
                              I Peter 5:14 (ASV)

The heart of every man seeks peace. What is peace?
It is "a togetherness of things that belong together."
(Rev. L. Verduin)

Now, what belongs together? God and His family.
Who belong to God's family? Those who love God and
God's law—His way *to* life and His way *for* life.

What is God's way to life? Jesus Christ who straight-
ened what was crooked by keeping God's law perfectly.
Those who come to God through Christ confessing that
they have rebelled against God's way and run away
from His family and now want to be taken back—to
such the Lord says, "Peace, you're back where you belong, My child. We belong together. Now live My way
(love my law) and you will never fall again (nothing
can make you stumble). I guarantee it."

Jesus Christ is the way to life, and His law is the way
for life. Should anything disrupt our togetherness with
God and thus disturb our peace, we would do well to
ask ourselves: "Am I somehow out of tune with Christ
or out of step with God's law? Do I hate someone that
I ought to love? Do I love something that I ought to
hate?"

Praise God for showing us the way to peace and help-
ing us to walk in it daily.

The Lord will give blessing and strength to His people,
The Lord all His people will comfort with peace.
                              Ps. 29 (metrical version)

24. PRAISE FOR SPRINGING WATER

"For with thee is the fountain of life. . ."
Ps. 36:9a (RSV)

"Look to him, and be radiant. . ."
Ps. 34:5a (RSV)

What is it to live? One of the common replies is: "Fear God and keep His commandments." I have often pondered the words "the fear of the Lord." I am steadily exploring the many ways in which that phrase is used in Scripture. I get to the point in my thinking where I am weighted down by my investigations. Then I end my pursuits temporarily and say to myself, "I must be on the wrong track; I don't think the 'fear of the Lord' is intended to be a weight on my mind but rather something to lift my spirit and to expand my outlook."

In one of those moments I caught myself singing:

> Thou of life, the fountain art,
> Freely let me take of thee;
> Spring thou up within my heart,
> Rise to all eternity.

In that moment I saw that surely part of "the fear of the Lord" is simply and steadily to become aware of who God is and what He does, and then to live more and more in the consciousness and the confidence that God is exactly what He says He is and that He does exactly what He promises. All I have to do is: "Look to him, and be radiant" (Ps. 34:5a). Or, in other words, to live, to be really alive, I must *look to God* so that I may *look like God.*

PRAYER:
Lord, help me to come alive today—to look to You and to radiate Your love and Your life. Open my eyes, Lord, and help me keep them open to the wonders of Your love so that I may point out such wonders to others and thus grow in "the fear of the Lord."

25. PRAISE FOR FOCUS AND FULLNESS

"I love thee, O Lord, my strength.
The Lord is my rock . . . my deliverer . . .
my God . . . my salvation. . ."
Ps. 18:1-2 (RSV)

Sometimes a timely remark in conversation will trigger a thought about our timeless God and give us another occasion for praise. I am not suggesting that we ought to read the Bible in the light of our experiences, but experiences can give us fresh insights into Biblical truths. And the Spirit often uses commonplace occurrences to sharpen our awareness and appreciation of our uncommon God.

I recently heard one friend remark to another, "I like that brooch. It's so striking with that suit." Now it happened that the person had had the brooch for years but had never worn it because the proper complementary attire was lacking. Similarly, I know of someone who found a picture she liked and in time built a room to fit the picture.

These illustrations suggest two ways of life: we can build God into our lives, or we can build our lives around God. The first is a form of idolatry, a patronizing way of recognizing God but still putting self and selfish ambitions in the center, the focal point. No praise to God can issue from such living. The second way—to build our lives around God—is God's way. It was the way the psalmist lived; and in that way, and that way only, he found the way to praise.

He found in God the unshakable ground of his being (my rock), the complete answer to all his needs (my deliverer), his unfailing sustenance (my strength), and his sure hope for a full life always (my salvation). No wonder he could say: "I love thee, O Lord . . . my God."

Praise God because He is God!

26. PRAISE FOR "A LETTER TO GOD"

"For the needy shall not always be forgotten,
and the hope of the poor shall not perish for ever."
                                    Ps. 9:18 (RSV)

The above prophecy of the psalmist is steadily being fulfilled. There is still so much to be done in bringing genuine, lasting hope to the poor, but there is also so much evidence of God's grace at work wherever men show His love.

The following expression of a hungry black youth from the Mississippi Delta reveals the amazing work of God's Spirit in giving many uneducated people unusual sensitivity and insight. This young man in speaking with a Christian relief worker was impressed by the costly love of God and expressed a desire to let God know of his own feelings. The worker invited the youth to write a letter to God. The idea excited him. He hurried to his room and wrote this piece:

Love is beautiful . . . Love is destruction.

Love is like seep water that slowly creeps up on its prey. It causes our bodies to be on guard and treat it special, but nevertheless we still lose our way . . .

Why is it that everybody loves something and loves to be loved back? . . .

I think that only the sensitive people really enjoy the full meaning of the thing, the beautiful and the destruction part, because maybe they like the tender touch and the terrible scar LOVE leaves on your heart.

                                    Dorsey Johnson (age 18)

What inquiry of spirit in this "letter"—so much awareness of the dilemma of man and the paradox of love! Praise God for such evidences of His grace! Is there, perhaps, a psalmist in the making in the Mississippi Delta? Pray God that it may be so. His promises are sure:

"The afflicted shall eat and be satisfied;
Those who seek him shall praise the Lord."
                                    Ps. 22:26 (RSV)

27. PRAISE FOR THE EAST WIND

"By means of the east wind
Thou breakest the ships of Tarshish."
Ps. 48:7 (Leupold)

The east wind blew all last night in many parts of our land. Today all roads are blocked with snow. No one can get out and go about his usual business. Schools are closed, meetings cancelled, and planes grounded.

There were decisions to be made today, transactions planned, cargo to be delivered, and so much work to be done. But the Lord of all spoke last night and said, "Stop! Sit still today. Think! Consider: are your ways my ways? Are your thoughts my thoughts? Are your plans my plans?"

The east wind is known for its destructive power. The ships of Tarshish were the mightiest sea-going vessels of those days. They represent anything that man might plan or make for his own pleasure or profit without thought whether his work would really please God and promote His cause more than anything else. Such self-serving structures God blows to bits.

But, usually the Lord does not let the east wind spend itself and wreck us. He often uses it to change the direction of our lives or send us back to harbor for a while.

Praise God for such east winds that cause us to "ponder anew what the Almighty can do."

28. PRAISE IN THE MORNING

"In his anger is disquiet, in his favour there is life.
Tears may linger at nightfall,
but joy comes in the morning."

Ps. 30:5 (NEB)

One of the delights of living in a family or with a companion is being greeted by a cheery "Good morning." Such a greeting is an indication of love and harmony. And such harmony produces joy and life; the lack of it brings forth discord and death.

The "sweet singer of Israel" knew this secret of life. He sang of it with an overflowing, thankful heart and invited all God's people ("his loyal servants" — Ps. 30:4a) to join with him in singing praises for the harmony that God has restored to us and for the joy that comes to us each day afresh because God chose to do us the favor of favors — to seize us from slipping into the Pit and to set our feet firmly on the path of life (Ps. 30:1-3).

There's an exciting discovery awaiting those who walk the path of life. We do not walk that path alone. Each step of the way we have a faithful, ever-refreshing Companion and a loving Teacher (Ps. 37:23, 24)

PRAYER:
O Lord, it's so good to be greeted by You in the morning. You strip off my sorrows and clothe me with joy. Help me to share that joy today, Lord, and to let someone know how great and good You are.

29. PRAISE AT NIGHT

And joyful meditations fill the watches of the night.
                                    Ps. 63 (metrical version)

Did you lie awake for a while last night? If so, what did you think about during that time?

In Psalm 63 David tells of his joyful musings during wakeful nights. (The word *meditate* in vs. 6 is used more like *muse*.) Such joy and peace at this time in David's life is really amazing. David was fleeing again. Whether he was hiding from Saul or from Absalom is not significant. The point is that David was running for his life once more, and stress and weariness flooded his soul. Take a moment to let your imagination play and picture David trying to sleep on a dry, dusty Judean hillside—no physical comforts and much emotional pain and mental strain. The "man after God's own heart," the anointed king of God's chosen people, is outcast, homeless, destitute.

But God's grace is stronger than the dread circumstances and once again lifts David above them. The ground on which David lies is hard, but the pillow of God's love is soft. The situation is uncertain, but the mercy of God is sure. And David, though wakeful, can rest. As he lies down, his thoughts drift. He draws on a storehouse of memories—so many times when God had proved Himself to be God, fully controlling all things and constantly loving His own. And as David in his loneliness snuggles up to God, God hugs David. Thus once again trouble produces blessing: weakness turns to strength, and struggle brings forth song.

PRAYER:
O God, teach us to gather substance for song during the day, whatever the time and the task may be, so that we may sing at night.

30. PRAISE FOR HIS GOODNESS

> *"O give thanks to the Lord, for he is good;*
> *for his steadfast love endures forever!*
> *Let the redeemed of the Lord say so. . . ."*
> Ps. 107:1-2a (RSV)

> *His goodness to me, his blessings so free*
> *I could not repay if I lived eternally;*
> *So I will use the life that He gave*
> *To tell the world of His goodness to me.*
> Louis Erwin

This lilting song expresses the oft-repeated feelings of the psalmist. How can this song become your song today and each day anew?

One of the first steps in cultivating a singing spirit and a life of praise is suggested throughout the psalms: "forget not . . . remember . . ." Psalms 103-107 are especially filled with such reminders.

But to remember, to call to mind the blessings the Lord has given—the specific instances and the unfailingness of God's goodness—takes time. It takes time to notice the evidences of God's work. It takes time to extract and to absorb from God's Word and from our experiences the sweetness of God's steadfast lovingkindness to us. Then it takes time to hold on to—to remember—God's ways in the past so that we may rejoice in Him today and trust Him for the future. And *it takes time to take time*. But if we order our days according to God's ways for our lives, we have time—time to notice, to extract, to absorb, and to remember.

There is so much wisdom in the old song:

> Take time to be holy;
> Speak oft with thy Lord.
> Abide in Him always
> And feed on His word . . .
>
> Take time to be holy
> The world rushes on . . .

Praise God for His goodness in giving us time to realize, to remember and to celebrate His goodness. Tell the world of it (Ps. 107:2a).

31. PRAISE FOR MAJESTY

*"O Jehovah, our Lord, how glorious
is Thy name in all the earth!
Thou hast displayed Thy majesty
above the heavens."*

Ps. 8:1 (NBV)

When the poet Hopkins looked at the night sky, he exploded with delight:

Look at the stars! look, look up at the skies!
O look at all the fire-folk sitting in the air!

Not everyone shares those sentiments, however. I know of a university student who is afraid to look at the stars. She said recently in a conversation with a friend, "I feel so small, so insignificant when I look up at night. I'm really frightened at the thought of how big the world is, how little the earth is in comparison with the universe, and what a tiny speck I am on this little earth. So, I dread to look at the sky at night. All the vastness and the grandeur pictured in the stars overwhelms me. It scares me. Where do I fit in all of this? Who cares about little me?"

The writer of Psalm 8 had some similar thoughts. But his response to the glories of creation was very different. He had the same question as the student: "When I observe . . . the moon and the stars . . ., what is man that Thou carest for him?" (vv. 3-4). But his answer speaks of awe and wonder, rather than in dread, of God. The difference lies in the blessed faith the psalmist enjoyed. By faith in Christ (Heb. 2:9), the psalmist saw the order of creation restored, and redeemed man, not cringing, but ruling (vv. 5-6).

We have but to ask for such faith to see beyond the stars and to catch daily glimpses of God's grand, mysterious plan for man—to lift him from the dust and to make of him a king. Hard to believe that, isn't it?

Praise God for His majesty—but also for your own!

32. PRAISE FOR THE SHEPHERD-KING

"He chose David to be his servant
and took him from the sheepfolds;
he brought him from minding the ewes
(that had young—RSV)
to be the shepherd of his people Jacob;
And he shepherded them in singleness of heart
and guided them with skilful hand."

Ps. 78:70-72 (NEB)

Could a farmer become President of our country? Sound ridiculous? It seems impossible in our complicated, manipulative society, but in the government of Israel, a shepherd became a king by God's direct selection.

Why a shepherd? The above text appears at the end of a psalm that records the faithfulness of God to Israel in spite of her unfaithfulness, and His steady care for her even when she showed no care for Him. To give Israel (and us) a living, visible demonstration of His care and His idea of a king, God picked a shepherd and put him on the throne. David, a shepherd boy, became God's "man of the hour." Because of Israel's plight and entanglement with many ungodly nations at the time, David had to be a fighting king. But in all his warring, he had the heart of a shepherd and ruled Israel with a shepherd's hand. In his governing, he was never out for his own glory but always sought the welfare of God's people and the honor of God's name.

Why a shepherd? A shepherd knew what it was to care for the weak—"to tend the ewes that had young" (v. 71, RSV) and to save lambs from the jaws of lions and bears (I Sam. 17:36). And David, the shepherd, knew that such compassion and strength came only from God, "the Lord of Hosts, the God of the army of Israel" (I Sam. 17:45).

Why a shepherd? Because David, the shepherd-king, pictured the reign of Christ, the Good Shepherd. And David shows us how we ought to live as shepherd-kings: care for the weak "in singleness of heart" and in complete reliance on the power of God.

33. PRAISE FOR PROVISION

"The Lord is my shepherd, I shall not want;
He makes me lie down in green pastures.
He leads me beside still waters,
He restores my soul."

Ps. 23:1-2 (RSV)

David's impressions of God as expressed in Psalm 23 have been the confession and comfort of God's people throughout the ages. He sees God as providing for His "sheep" in every way and giving them a sense of adequacy so that they can function fully—carry out God's purposes in this world.

"I shall not want." There is freedom from physical want because of the abundant provision of God. "He makes me lie down in green pastures." There is much to feed on both physically and spiritually.

"He restores my soul." There is full provision for the spirit of man. There are disappointments, adversities, frustrations, and unattained goals in the lives of all of us daily, but the Lord provides restoration in His time and way. Often an unexpected visit, call, or letter from a friend will be God's way of "giving us a lift."

"He leads me beside still waters." The Good Shepherd also provides a sense of tranquility so that we can cope with the heat and the stress of the day.

This ancient confession fits our contemporary needs. In times of shaky economics, crumbling governments, threats of famine and overwhelming powers, we can have the inner calm that David experienced when we know David's God—the complete, unfailing Provider of all our needs. And we can sing:

> "The King of Love my Shepherd is,
> Whose goodness faileth never;
> I nothing lack if I am his and
> He is mine for ever."

34. PRAISE FOR ASSIGNMENT

"The Lord is my shepherd . . .
He leads me beside still waters . . .
He leads me in paths of righteousness
for his name's sake."
                    Ps. 23:1a, 2b, 3b (RSV)

There is so much comfort and thought for praise in the old hymn:

He leadeth me; O blessed thought!
O words with heavenly comfort fraught!
Whate'er I do, where'er I be,
Still 'tis God's hand that leadeth me.
                    Joseph H. Gilmore

We need the steady reassurance of God's providing, protecting, and preserving hand. We need to know that the Lord shepherds us—that He provides food and constant care.

But then this faith in a caring God must be translated into action. The provision is a preparation for service. "He leads me in paths of righteousness for his name's sake" (v. 3b). There is the leading but also the obedient following. There is rest so that we may walk. There is divine caring for us so that we may show care for others.

Where are "the paths of righteousness"? Where is God's name to be made known? Wherever there is need —lack of food, justice, courage, health—or whatever the need may be. There is so much work to be done. There are so many people who do not know the care and the healing touch of the Good Shepherd. And some who do, need reassurance.

PRAYER:
Lord, show me who needs Your care today and help me to care for them as You would. With one hand in Yours, may I reach out the other hand to others. And accept my praise as I sing:

His faithful follower I would be,
For by His hand He leadeth me.

35. PRAISE FOR GOD'S COMPANIONSHIP

"Even though I walk through the valley
of the shadow of death,
I fear no evil; for thou art with me."
Ps. 23:4a (RSV)

There are the shadows in life. They are part of the fabric of everyone's experience, though the lives of some seem to be darker than others. But the shadows of hardship for God's people are far outshadowed by God's ever-present companionship. Trouble casts a shadow, but the shade of God's love is so much bigger than the shape of any difficulty.

Eliphaz said to Job: "Man is born to trouble as the sparks fly upward" (Job 5:7, RSV). These words are not true for those who know the companionship of the Lord and walk close to Him. It is true, of course, that God's children suffer much and troubles fall upon them almost daily, sometimes almost relentlessly. But difficulties do not overwhelm or overpower us if we confess "The Lord is my shepherd." Such a "safety margin" is not because of any special inherent strength or any particular exercise of the will—the ability to "grin and bear it" or to "keep your chin up." The secret of our "bearing up" is not in us but in God who "bears us up" (Ps. 145:14). Or, in the words of Psalm 23: "I fear no evil, *for thou art with me."* Though David's life was full of trouble and he seemed to go from one crisis to another, he walked unafraid because he knew God was with him. And that steady assurance of God's ever-watchful presence kept David steady.

We have all experienced how fear disappears when someone who loves us is with us. God loves us. God is with us. Praise God for His loving companionship. Walk close to God—in sun or in shadow, for "no good thing does the Lord withhold from those who walk uprightly" (Ps. 84:11b, RSV).

36. PRAISE FOR GOD'S HOSPITALITY

"Thou preparest a table before me
in the presence of my enemies,
Thou anointest my head with oil; my cup overflows."
Ps. 23:5 (RSV)

The invitations are out. The guests are invited not only to the ceremony but also to the celebration which is to follow. We are all acquainted with this procedure in our day.

There are some parallels between our feasts and the banquet of which David speaks in the above text. First of all, there is a host who attends to all the preparations and supplies all the food. (*"Thou* preparest. . . .") And if the host is worthy of his name, he is gracious, genial, and generous. In David's experience the Lord is such a host: the table is well spread, the atmosphere is fragrant (anointing oil), and the refreshments are super-abundant (an overflowing cup).

And then there are guests. Some are invited and some are not. There are those who participate in the feast, and there are those who stand outside: the "enemies," malicious persons who envy the happiness of the guests and desire to rob them of their joy.

Is there unjust discrimination in this feast? Why are some invited and others not? The fact is that no one deserves an invitation. No one is a special friend of the Shepherd-Host. But those who see how much they need all that the Good Shepherd offers them have learned one word that makes them God's friends and gives them the right to eat at God's table. And that word is GRACE—the undeserved love of God in Christ. Grace, and grace alone, qualifies us to enjoy God's prepared table.

Finally, there is "entertainment" at this banquet: the opportunity to enjoy the company of our gracious Host and to thank Him over and over for His abundant grace. Enjoy God today and always!

37. PRAISE FOR OPTIMISM

"Surely goodness and mercy shall follow me
all the days of my life:
And I shall dwell in the house of the Lord for ever."
Ps. 23:6 (RSV)

What is the climax of all the blessings enjoyed when one is shepherded daily by the Lord, the only true God? It is a true, deep, and real friendship with God. Words cannot express the intimacy a child of God experiences with his Father God. We use various words: companionship, fellowship, communion. Analyze each one, find the root meanings of each, study the synonyms, add them all up and you will begin to see what friendship with God is — what life really is.

To enjoy close friendship with God in the present we, like David, need to look back and look ahead. David's confidence rests on past experiences and on the sure promises of God. Though David had much trouble and sometimes even felt that the Lord had forsaken him (Ps. 22:1), he still testified that "goodness and mercy" had been his lot. And his cries for help end with praise for deliverance.

Not all of his perplexities were removed, however. And from this we learn the need for faith in the promises of God but, more than that, faith in the One who promised and remains faithful. David had the confidence that God always does what He says He's going to do.

With that resolute confidence he could look forward to the future with optimism and hope. He knew that the God who gave life also sustains life. He knew that nothing could thwart the purpose of God in making man to be His friend and in redeeming the life of man to enjoy life with God.

"I shall not die, but I shall live,
and recount the deeds of the Lord."
Ps. 118:17, (RSV)

38. PRAISE FOR PREPARATION

"He taught Moses to know his way."
Ps. 103:7a (NEB)

Did it ever strike you that the men and women noted in Scripture as heroes of faith and leaders of God's people never applied for a job? They were sought out by the Lord, sent to His school, and then commissioned in His time and way.

Take Moses as an example. His mother was his first teacher, and Pharaoh's daughter had him educated in all the knowledge of the Egyptians. At the end of that training Moses had big ideas of what he might do for his people. But God said, "No, Moses, the diplomas of Egypt do not certify you for My service. You must know not only the Egyptian ways but also My way. And to teach you that way, I'm going to send you to the desert to take care of sheep for forty years." As the psalmist records: "He taught Moses to know his way."

David, too, was prepared by God to be the leader of God's people at a critical time in their history. Before God called him, David knew the ways of sheep (Ps. 78:70-72), he knew how to fight their enemies (I Sam. 17:34-36), and he had learned the source of his strength: "The Lord who delivered me from the paw of the lion and from the paw of the bear will deliver me from the hand of this Philistine" (I Sam. 17:37).

The Lord equipped both these men with sensitive souls and poetic minds so that life's experiences were etched on their hearts. Then out of it all God caused poetry and music to flow from their pens and tongues. The lives of these shepherd-warriors still instruct us that "all of life is a preparation," and their songs inspire us to sing with new insight:

Lead on, O King Eternal, the day of march has come . . .
Through years of preparation Thy grace has made us strong,
And now, O King Eternal, we lift our battle song.

Ernest W. Shurtloff, 1887

39. PRAISE FOR WORK IN TIME

"So teach us to number our days
that we may get a heart of wisdom.
Let the favor of the Lord be upon us,
and establish thou the work of our hands."
Ps. 90:12, 17 (RSV)

The eternal God, who has neither beginning of days nor end of life, still works in time and works progressively in time.

In Psalm 90, Moses reflects on the wonders of the timeless God who moves in time and gives man time to do His work. Moses was very much aware of his need for daily wisdom and for God's blessing to make every day of his life count for God. Read his prayer again.

But recognize as you read that we live in an era far richer than the days of Moses. We need the same wisdom and blessing for which Moses prayed; but that Wisdom has come in the person of Christ, and the blessing Moses sought has been poured out on God's people since Pentecost. Thus we who confess Christ need no longer to plead as Moses did. We have only to ask God to open our eyes to realize the grandeur of our position — partners with Christ — and the limitlessness of our resources — heirs of the Spirit. With such a vision, we need to sit down together ("teach *us*") to figure out ways to make every day a new day — a day in which we gladly and purposefully set out to do what God tells us needs doing in the world today. When we are in tune with what God wants to do through us, the favor of the Lord will be upon us and our work will stand (v. 17).

Praise God for work — His work for us, in us, and through us.

40. PRAISE FOR ACCEPTANCE

"Sing his praise in the assembly of the faithful . . .
For the Lord accepts the service of his people."
Ps. 149:1b, 4a (NEB)

We've all had an occasion for giving a gift to some-one. When the gift is received with genuine pleasure (it seems to be something really appreciated), the giver is very glad to be the means of making someone happy; and the receiver is glad for the giver's thoughtfulness.

The same reciprocal action takes place between the Lord God and those who praise Him. Praising God is like giving God a gift that really pleases Him. He extends the invitation to praise, gives man the grace to see the reasons for praise, and then sits back with sheer joy to see man respond to His gracious invitation and His works of grace. No, He doesn't really *sit back* and enjoy man's gift of thankful praise; He actively accepts (receives) man's praises. It is as if the mighty Father God sits down right beside His children when they give Him praise and says to them, "I'm so glad with your gift. It just thrills Me to hear you sing. You couldn't have given Me anything that would please Me more."

Isn't it amazing that the God who created and sustains all that is and "owns the cattle on a thousand hills" still has such a big heart and magnanimous spirit that He smiles as He listens to His singing children and says, "To hear you sing makes Me so happy. Sing another song for Me."

And man's heart is so warmed to know that his God accepts his gift that his soul sings ever more freely, and he keeps on dreaming up new ways to please God with gifts of praise.

41. PRAISE FOR WRESTLING

"Why are the nations in turmoil?
Why do the peoples hatch their futile plots?"
Ps. 2:1 (NEB)

"Why stand so far off, Lord,
hiding thyself in time of need?"
Ps. 10:1 (NEB)

These texts could have been taken from today's newspaper. The turmoil among nations, the futility of men's plans, and the desperate needs throughout the world distress us. And we stand with the psalmist in perplexity. We identify with his cries of "Why?" and "How long?"

Yet we rejoice in the results of the psalmist's wrestling. In reading the record of his struggles, we enter into the stern realities of life, share the depths of his experience, and rise with him to new heights of insight and vision. Without such wrestling, the psalms would be only a kind of anecdotal record, interesting to look at, like an exhibit in a museum. Because the psalms portray genuine struggles, they are much more than a collector's item on display. They provide an indispensable map and guidebook for travelers (pilgrims) of all times seeking to walk God's way every day. As we become intimately acquainted with the psalms and the Lord God who inspired them, we perceive the difference between *collecting* ideas and *wrestling* with them.

Praise God for the wrestlings revealed in the psalms!

PRAYER:
And help us, God, to put away our childish practices of "collecting." Give us the courage to raise questions, to face issues, to challenge the wiles of the evil one in the world of ideas.

42. PRAISE FOR STRENGTH
FROM PROMISES

"Now when David and his men came to Ziklag . . . they found it burned with fire, and their wives and sons and daughters taken captive. Then David and the people who were with him raised their voices and wept, until they had no more strength to weep . . . And David was greatly distressed; for the people spoke of stoning him, because all the people were bitter in soul, each for his sons and daughters. But David strengthened himself in the Lord his God."

I Sam. 30:1, 3, 4, 6 (RSV)

That last sentence can be the basis for extended meditation. The rest of the story is this: David consulted God by means of the ephod, and God told David to pursue the enemy, promising him victory. David went forth in the strength of that promise. And the victory was his.

Today we have no ephod as David had, but consultation with the Lord is just as real and His voice is just as clear. The resources are there. All we have to do is tap them—or, as Isaiah expressed it, "draw water out of the wells of salvation" (Isa. 12:3a, ASV).

We have a Book of promises. It is up to us to claim them—to cash in on them. We often sing: "Standing on the promises of Christ my King." But how many promises do we actually know? How much of this Book is a living part of us?

I invite you to try what I consider to be a refreshing and stimulating spiritual exercise, one of the ways of "strengthening ourselves in the Lord." Search the Bible for God's promises and each day memorize one. In the next four pages I will name only a few promises from psalms in Scripture and suggest a thought from each. I recommend that you take up the devotional exercise from there: find a promise, learn it by *heart*, and *stand* on it.

43. PRAISE FOR GOD'S ARMS

*"The eternal God is your dwelling place,
and underneath are the everlasting arms."*
Deut. 33:27a (RSV)

The psalms of Scripture are not limited to the Book of *Psalms*. Moses wrote and sang psalms, two of which are recorded for us in Deuteronomy (Chap. 32 and 33). In his beautiful psalm of farewell and final blessings to Israel, he spoke words of comfort that have sustained God's people all through the years and through many a troubled day.

Read the above text again. Read it aloud. Note the nouns: God, dwelling-place (home), arms. Note the adjectives: eternal, everlasting. And then note the word *underneath*—a word used to show a relationship. Many of the promises of God deal with His relationships to His people.

Moses pictures God here as the God who stands outside of time yet all during the time of our lives and at every time His all-powerful, steadying arms are underneath us. (Note well: not *beneath* but *underneath*.)

Underneath—what a world of comfort is wrapped up in that one word. God is underneath. That means that even when the bottom of our lives seems to have dropped out, God is still there. He is under the bottom— "underneath are the everlasting arms." And that's real. God says so, and I've found it so. And so have many of you.

Praise God for His everlasting arms *underneath*.

> Thine arm, O Lord, in days of old
> Was strong to heal and save . . .
> Be Thou our great Deliverer still,
> Thou Lord of life and death . . .
> *E. H. Plumptre, 1866*

44. PRAISE FOR GOD'S EMBRACE

"As the mountains are round about Jerusalem,
so the Lord is round about his people,
from this time forth and for evermore."

Ps. 125:2 (RSV)

This text always brings to my mind a picture of my homeland—a broad valley entirely surrounded by mountains. There is something solid and protective about a mountain, and the psalmist uses it as a figure to picture the steadfastness of God and the complete security of His people.

To catch more of the beauty and the power of the comparisons to mountains in Psalm 125:1-2, we ought to imagine people on a pilgrimage to Jerusalem. As they walked along, they first caught sight of the hills before they saw the city. From a distance these hills looked like one big mountain to those walking along the plains. This mighty mountain, Mount Zion (v. 1), was rooted in the bedrock of the earth and thus suggested unshaken solidity.

As the travelers approached the city and came to the top of the hills, they saw the city nestled in them and surrounded by their protection. And that view pictures the constant enfolding love of God as He stands "round about" His people and embraces those who trust Him, those who depend on Him and on Him alone.

That is the key to the comfort in this promise—trust.

O God of the mountains, help us to believe unquestionably that, even if the mountains should move, You are immovable; and thus those who trust in You cannot be moved and may always know the snug security of Your impenetrable embrace.

"All who, with heart confiding, depend on God alone,
Like Zion's mount abiding, shall ne'er be overthrown.
Like Zion's city, bounded by guarding mountains broad,
His people are surrounded forever by their God."

Ps. 125 (metrical version)

45. PRAISE FOR THE GOD WITHIN

"The Lord loves the gates of Zion . . .
and he has made her his home."
Ps. 87:1, 4 (NEB)

We sing:

> Zion, founded on the mountains,
> God, thy maker, loves thee well;
> He has chosen thee, most precious,
> He delights in thee to dwell.

Isn't it amazing that the God who has promised always to be "underneath" us and "round about" us also lives within us and works through us? The psalmist makes clear that Zion—the church of God—is the place where God is pleased to live, and the house that God calls home is the heart of anyone who finds his home in God. Oh, what a salvation is this, that God lives in me!

This promise (fact) was celebrated by David and other psalmists, but the fullness of its comfort and power became known only through Christ's work on earth and at Pentecost. We recall some of the parting words of Jesus: "And I will pray the Father, and he will give you another Comforter, to be with you forever, even the Spirit of truth . . . he dwells with you and will be in you" (John 14:16, 17). After the Spirit had come on the church and in the hearts and lives of all believers, the same writer (John) could give these words of assurance: ". . . he who is in you is greater than he who is in the world" (I John 4:4b, RSV).

The God within rids us of futility and weakness and fills us with purpose and power. He not only comforts us with His presence but also challenges us to demonstrate who He is and what He does.

O God within us, may it be said of us, as it was of the singer of Israel's psalms: "the spirit of the Lord has spoken through me" (II Sam. 23:4, NEB).

46. PRAISE TO THE GOD ABOVE

*"Show thyself, O God, high above the heavens;
let thy glory shine over all the earth."*

Ps. 57:5 (NEB)

There is the God *above*—the God beyond—who is
directing all life's events and preparing all things for
His return. For the expression of that promise and the
culmination of all promises, we join in the song of
Isaiah—a song of exaltation, of hope, and of heaven.

> He will swallow up death for ever, and the Lord God
> will wipe away tears from all faces, and the reproach of
> his people he will take away from all the earth; for the
> Lord has spoken.
>
> It will be said on that day, "Lo, this is our God; we
> have waited for him, that he might save us. This is the
> Lord; we have waited for him; let us be glad and re-
> joice in his salvation." (Isa. 25:8, 9, RSV)

Do we believe this? Yes, we do, don't we? Then,
"let us be glad and rejoice in his salvation" and, like
David, "strengthen ourselves in the Lord" and praise
our God, who is underneath, around, within, and above
His people. His promises are ours. We have only to find
them and to claim them. They will be our armor by
day and our pillow at night.

> King of glory, reign forever,
> Thine an everlasting crown;
> Nothing from thy love shall sever
> Those whom thou hast made thine own,
> Happy objects of thy grace,
> Destined to behold thy face.
> Alleluia! Alleluia!
> Alleluia! Amen.

Thomas Kelly

47. PRAISE FOR MERCIFUL CAPTIVITY

"Great is thy mercy, O Lord; give me life. . ."
Ps. 119:156 (RSV)

"Thou didst ascend . . . leading captives. . ."
Ps. 68:18a (RSV)

What is life? When are we really living? According to Psalm 119, Psalm 73:27-28, and many other references in Scripture, *the first step toward life is to admit death—to come to God and say, "O God, I'm dying! Without* You I'm worthless and life is senseless. Give me life!"

Then God in mercy takes firm hold of us (captures us, Ps. 68:18) and begins to instruct us: "Yes, I know. Now listen to me. You are my child. I made you and have come to reclaim you and redirect you. The road that you are traveling will lead to a *pit* of waste and destruction (Ps. 73:18). I will show you a path that leads to a *hill* of worth and fulfillment" (Ps. 16:11).

When we first feel God's hand on our lives and hear His voice, we resist and want to talk back. But His tones quiet us. We listen more closely as He continues. "And now I am attaching to you an unbreakable cord which I made myself. It cost me my life. This cord is LOVE. It will be as a brand on you, and anyone seeing the blood-stained cord will recognize you as my property. This cord keeps you close to me, but at the same time it will give you a freedom which you have never known before" (cf. Ps. 116:16).

We are beginning to understand, but the question persists: How can one really live if he is bound? God's property! Captives! There is something repulsive about the thought. We want to be free—to be ourselves. But as the Captor continues to reveal Himself and His purposes to us, we begin to see that only as His captives can we be our true selves—free representatives of a merciful God.

"And I will walk at liberty
because thy truth I seek . . ."
Ps. 119 (metrical version)

48. PRAISE FOR THE BREATH OF GOD

> *"The very word of David . . .*
> *the singer of Israel's psalms:*
> *'The spirit of the Lord*
> *has spoken through me . . .'"*
> II Sam. 23:1-2 (NEB)

A life of praise is sustained by the breath of inspiration. This is true for everyone who would praise God and lead others to praise.

Picture yourself as a guide leading a group of hikers on a mountain climb. You, the guide, must blaze the trail and point out the grand views as you climb. You begin the hike with vigor, but soon you are out of breath. How senseless it would be to keep on climbing! Without breath you cannot go on; and without you, others may not find the way and discover the hidden delights. There is no other way to accomplish your purpose—you must take time to catch your breath.

So it is with a life of praise. It takes "breath" to walk on ahead, to point out the beauty along the way, and to lead the way to the top. Those who really want to praise God "every day in every way" need to be inspired—"breathed into"—by the Spirit of the living God, the Breath that prompts and sustains praise. It was the Spirit of the Lord that prompted David to compose and to sing songs of praise. It is that same Spirit that inspires us to sing and uses our singing lives to inspire others to praise.

Inspiration is mysterious but practical. We do not know all the mysteries of the work of the Spirit, but we know that He uses means—"fresh air" and exercise in prayerful reading and observing, conversing, reflection and recreation. There is real effort involved, but without it no one can lead a life of praise.

> Breathe on me, Breath of God
> Fill me with life anew,
> That I may love what thou dost love,
> And do what thou wouldst do.
> *Elwin Hatch*

49. PRAISE FOR A CHARGE TO KEEP

"He laid on Jacob a solemn charge . . .
to teach their sons . . ."
Ps. 78:5 (NEB)

The Spirit of God imparts not only breath and energy but also illumination and insight. And through Him the Christian catches a vision of his place and his work in this world—of what it means to have "a charge to keep."

John Hersey in a book titled *The Child Buyer* pictures a man who is scouting America for talented youth. His business is to buy gifted children and train them as research scientists for the advancement of his selfish interests. His chief pitch is "I buy brains." There is something in this statement that incenses the heart of a Christian. It offends his sense of trusteeship. He replies with holy anger: "Brains are not for sale. Neither are children to be made ready for the markets of this world." *Brains*, or whatever the gift may be, *are not a commodity* to be purchased by men *but a trust* to be used for God.

There is a divine order of work under which a Christian operates. God is supreme—the Creator, the Savior, and the Master. He made man, redeemed him, and commissioned him. The Lord God has a program—to make His truth known and to reclaim the world. To accomplish this work, He commissions redeemed men and gives them the capital necessary to carry out His business. Then, as He did in the days of Israel recorded by the psalmist, He specifies the laws of operation: trust, remember, obey, and *"tell* to the coming generation *the glorious deeds of the Lord"* (Ps. 78:4, 7).

> Tell of His wondrous works, tell of His glory,
> Til through the nations His name is revered;
> Praise and exalt Him, for He is almighty,
> God over all, let the Lord be feared.
> *Ps. 96 (metrical version)*

50. PRAISE BY RECEIVING AND GIVING

"What shall I render unto Jehovah
for all his benefits . . . ?
I will take the cup of salvation . . .
I will offer to thee the sacrifice
of thanksgiving. . ."
Ps. 116:12, 13a, 17a (ASV)

There are two seas in Palestine. One is fresh, and fish are in it. Splashes of green adorn its banks. Trees spread their branches over it, and stretch out their thirsty roots to sip of its healing water. Along its shores the children play.

The River Jordan makes this sea with sparkling water from the hills. So it laughs in the sunshine. And men build their houses near to it, and birds their nests; and every kind of life is happier because it is there.

The River Jordan flows on south into another sea. Here is no splash of fish, no fluttering leaf, no song of birds, no children's laughter. Travelers choose another route, unless on urgent business. . . What makes this mighty difference in these neighbor seas? Not the River Jordan. It empties the same good water into both. Not the soil in which they lie; not the country round about.

This is the difference: The Sea of Galilee receives but does not keep the Jordan. For every drop that flows into it another drop flows out. *The giving and receiving go on in equal measure.* The other sea is shrewder, hoarding its income jealously . . . Every drop it gets, it keeps. The Sea of Galilee gives and lives. The other sea gives nothing. It is named the Dead.

There are two seas in Palestine. There are two kinds of people in the world. Which kind are we?

This bit of poetic prose by an unknown author emphasizes so well that something must flow from our lives. The psalmist noted even more aptly that we must first receive before we can give and God is praised by our receiving—taking His salvation first and then sharing it.

51. PRAISE FOR THE MINISTRY OF ANGELS

"For he has charged his angels
to guard you wherever you go."
Ps. 91:11 (NEB)

Last week near midnight our quiet neighborhood was disturbed by a strange voice coming over a loud-speaker and threatening, "You are completely surrounded! Don't move. You are completely surrounded!" Since there was no one in sight, the people in my house decided it was the voice of a prankster.

But when God says, "You are completely surrounded," there is only comfort in His tones. I wonder, though, how seriously we take His words. How often do we reflect upon the constant watchfulness and the steady guarding ministry of the angels? Oh, yes, we think about such care when we have narrowly escaped injury or have been spared some pending disaster, such as a serious illness or a destructive storm. But do we remember to praise God for His daily, moment-by-moment care administered by the angels?

Perhaps we do not praise God more for His angels because we are often unaware of the evil forces surrounding us and steadily enticing us to "let down our guard." What are the things that wear down our spiritual vitality, that slowly but surely dull our sensitivities to sin? What are we doing to keep our senses keen so that we can see a "fowler's snare" (Ps. 91:3), "the hunters' trap" (v. 5), or the snakes in our path (v. 13)?

Only those who sense their peril will run for their lives to the shelter that God provides (v. 1). Then, to those who have found safety in God (v. 9), the Lord God says, "Now my angels will keep you wherever you go. You can't be hurt when you are on a mission for me because you are 'completely surrounded' by guarding angels."

Blessed be God—the God of the angels!

52. PRAISE FOR SOMETHING TO SAY

"O Lord, open thou my lips,
and my mouth shall show forth thy praise."
Ps. 51:15 (RSV)

In a small cafe in Northern Minnesota sat three men engaged in high-spirited conversation. Since my back was turned toward them, I had no idea of their physical appearance; but I could not help overhearing their talk. They revealed in the first few sentences that they were leaders of the Jaycee Convention going on in that town. But the business of the convention and the challenge of proper guidance for young men seemed not to be their first interest, for their conversation soon turned to matters of food and drink, particularly the latter. For at least twenty minutes they discussed enthusiastically the calories in a glass of beer, how one could adjust a diet for the relief of a heart condition so that he could still indulge in his regular beer intake and favorite mixed-drink recipes. As they talked, I thought, "That's the world—nothing to talk about but the satisfaction of sensual appetites."

But, what do we Christians talk about? I invite you to check. Is it true that about 90 per cent of all conversation—even among Christians—concerns clothes, houses, cars, physical pleasures, and the affairs of others? Are we all perhaps somewhat like Gratiano in *The Merchant of Venice*, who is characterized as speaking "an infinite deal of nothing"? How much of our talk is mere vanity—flat, superficial, worthless?

When we, like David, know God and the joys of salvation, we have something to say. And we praise God for real substance in speech.

My mouth shall show before the world
The glory of thy Name.
Ps. 51 (metrical version)

53. PRAISE WITH SPARKLING SPEECH

"May my teaching drop as the rain,
my speech distil as the dew. . ."
Deut. 32:2a (RSV)

". . . my lips will praise thee."
Ps. 63:3b (RSV)

There is nothing more attractive than beautiful, flowing speech. In his farewell song to Israel, Moses invited their attention with these words: "My speech [shall] distil as the dew." *As the dew*—sparkling, refreshing, enhancing! Have you ever walked through a woods, a pasture, or even your own backyard in the early morning while the dew was still on the grass and the flowers? Every blade and petal glistened with freshness, and you took a few deep breaths to take in something of the purity and beauty of your surroundings. You felt uplifted, renewed, exhilarated.

The speech of the redeemed should have a similar delightful effect. We are representatives of a beautiful Savior and a resplendent King. Let our conversation then be worthy of Him—attractive, flavored with discretion and humor, worthwhile, and winning. And as the dew which falls from above revives the earth daily, so may our everyday speech find its source in heavenly fountains and supply refreshment to all—even to those who oppose us. In this way we can be attractive, convincing witnesses to the grace and power of God and praise Him as we ought.

Again the psalmist leads the way:

Because thy tender love I see,
More precious far than life to me,
My lips shall praise thy grace.
Ps. 63 (metrical version)

54. PRAISE FROM A FRUITFUL TREE

> *Blest is he who loves God's precepts,*
> *Who from sin restrains his feet. . . .*
>
> *He is like a tree well planted*
> *By the flowing river's side,*
> *Ever green of leaf and fruitful—*
> *Thus shall all his works abide.*
> Ps. 1 (metrical version)

What joyous words! Anyone who hates sin and loves God is "like a tree planted by streams of water" (Ps. 1:3a, RSV). A tree that is planted by God Himself will surely grow. The evidence of deep roots and steady growth is unmistakable: constantly green leaves and everbearing fruit.

One of the most picturesque, poetic commentaries on Psalm 1 and the life of a person who is rooted in God and feeds on God's supplies was written by the prophet Jeremiah:

> "Blessed is the man who trusts in the Lord,
> whose trust is the Lord.
> He is like a tree planted by water,
> that sends out its roots by the stream,
> and does not fear when heat comes,
> for its leaves remain green,
> and is not anxious in the year of drought,
> for it does not cease to bear fruit."
> Jer. 17:7-8 (RSV)

How can we be sure that our lives will never wilt but will always be luxuriantly green and fruitful? If our *taproot* is planted deep (Ps. 84:5a) and constantly growing deeper into the very source of all life—Jesus Christ (Eph. 3:17-19), we will enjoy the steady refreshment and invigoration of "living water" (John 4:10).

Praise God for a resplendent life—a life like a tree: planted by God, rooted in Christ, nourished by living waters, and loaded with fruit—fruit to give away for the refreshment and healing (salvation) of others (Rev. 22:1-2).

55. PRAISE WITH A NEW SONG

"Sing a new song to the Lord . . .
Declare among the nations, 'The Lord is King . . .
He will judge the peoples justly . . .'"
$\qquad\qquad\qquad\qquad\qquad$ Ps. 96:1a, 10 (NEB)

A new song? What was the old one? The same one we hear and sing so often today. The old song speaks of power, and its singers make an idol out of external strength. Like Israel, we want security and we count our money, build our armies, and stockpile our supply of weapons. We compare our forces and our resources with those of other nations and steadily check on our standing as a world power. And other nations do the same. Oh, the song is old, and the pitch is false.

The psalmist says, "Let's get in tune with the truth! God alone gives strength. The Lord is King! And His kingdom is not a display of earthly power and pride but a demonstration of heavenly justice and mercy. He is a Shepherd-King. His aim is not to lord it over others but to lead them out. 'His law is love and His gospel is peace.'"

Oh, sing a new song—a song to a King who has a special concern for those who have a special need. Sing of the King of love, who came to earth with justice in His hand and mercy in His heart and is coming again to right all wrongs.

PRAYER:
O God, our King, we praise You for Your saving concern for us. Now help us to be in tune with Your plan for redeeming the world in mercy and ruling it with justice here and now. May we be done with building power at the expense of others and begin spending ourselves to help them so that our songs may ring true.

56. PRAISE FOR HOPE

Oh, my soul, why art thou grieving?
What disquiets and dismays?
Hope in God; His help receiving,
I shall yet my Savior praise.
  Ps. 43 (refrain of metrical version)

I find myself singing this refrain so often when I am inclined to fret or worry. Sometimes I'm humming the tune or singing the song almost unconsciously. Then suddenly the truth of what I'm saying hits me. My fears are gone, and my spirit is lifted.

The writer of Psalms 42 and 43 is troubled to the point of depression. He feels as though God has forsaken him and that he will never again experience the blessedness of knowing that God is near and that God is leading him every step of the way. He recalls the days when he celebrated his faith—when he participated in the festivals of praise and led the processional to the house of God, shouting and singing praise all along the way (42:4). And then he cries out: "O God, will I ever be happy again? Are my days of celebration ended?" In response to that cry, the Lord sends light and cheer and reminds the despondent one that He, the Lord, is still there and His ways haven't changed (42:8). The Lord seems to say in the background: "Leave all your questions with Me. Use Me, the Light, to dispel your darkness. Believe in Me, the Truth, to keep men's falsehood from hurting you. And then you'll be back in the procession of praise again."

To that the psalmist says, "O God, You're so right! Oh, send out Your light and Your truth. Let them lead me so that I may always live with You."

And *that's hope*—to know that God's light and truth, His cheering and unfailing love, will lead us home— home to stay!

57. PRAISE FOR THE LISTENING WIND

"Praise the Lord from the earth . . .
stormy wind fulfilling his command."
Ps. 148:7a, 8 (RSV)

"Listen to the wind." That is a rather common, but intriguing, invitation that may give us unusual sensations. When we are safe at home, we listen comfortably. When we are out in the storm, especially when we are on the water, we listen fearfully. In either case, we are the listeners, and the wind passes by.

The psalmist changes the order of the imperative and addresses himself to the wind. He says, "Listen, wind, to your Maker. By listening to Him (fulfilling his command), you will praise Him."

What is a listening wind, and how does it speak praise or help us to praise? In the context of the above text, a listening wind seems to be a potentially destructive wind sent by God to remind man of God's judgments upon man's sin.

"Fire and hail, snow and frost, stormy wind . . ." All of these elements suggest danger—overwhelming forces in life. But read on: "stormy wind *fulfilling his command*" ("obeying his voice," NEB). Ah, there it is—the listening wind—wind that is always under God's control. It comes and goes at God's command! And in its response to God's voice, the wind praises God. It reveals God's power *and mercy*.

PRAYER:
O God, the stormy winds are so real, but we praise You that You are Lord of the storm—that the wind listens to You.

58. PRAISE FOR A SENSE OF VALUES

Though in life he (mortal man) wealth attained,
Though the praise of men he gained,
He shall join those gone before,
Where the light shall shine no more.
Crowned with honor though he be,
Highly gifted, strong and free,
If he be not truly wise,
Man is like the beast that dies.

Ps. 49:18-20 (metrical version)

Have you ever thought of what might be engraved on your tombstone if God Himself were to write it? A possible epitaph a psalmist suggests is: "He lived and died like a senseless beast." Makes you shudder, doesn't it? In Psalm 49 God tells us with shocking directness that there is only one way to live so that we may enjoy God now and always. Any deviation from this way makes man live as a fool and die like a dog.

God is realistic. And His Word cuts through all of our pretenses, our rationalizing, our compromising, or whatever we may be using to avoid facing God and living a life worthy of man as a crown prince (or princess) in God's kingdom.

What are some of the misleading, corrupting powers that make us more like fools and beasts than like the truly wise people we were meant to be? The fool's ways are clearly set forth in Psalm 49. In his heart a fool really trusts himself or something else more than God. He expends his energies for personal gain: more land, a better house, bigger "toys," a more-recognized position, and more opportunities to make himself look big or good.

PRAYER:
O God, some of these desires are in *me*! Deliver me from my folly. Make me truly wise: to know what really counts in life and to show this sense of values consistently. May my epitaph read: "She lived and died as a child of God."

59. PRAISE FOR VICTORY THROUGH GRACE

"The Lord will give strength to his people."
Ps. 29:11a (NEB)
"Jehovah will give grace and glory. . ."
Ps. 84:11b (ASV)

Praise God with a sense of victory today! An old hymn expresses it so well:

> Conquering now and still to conquer,
> Rideth a King in His might,
> Leading the host of all the faithful
> Into the midst of the fight;
> See them with courage advancing,
> Clad in their brilliant array,
> Shouting the name of their Leader,
> Hear them exaltingly say:
> "Not to the strong is the battle,
> Not to the swift is the race,
> Yet to the true and the faithful
> Victory is promised through grace."

Yes, life with God is victorious! The psalmists could tell of many deliverances and sing of many victories. But they lived only in the prospect of the coming Messiah. We live in the day of fulfilled hopes. How much surer should be our confidence in God and how much grander our view of life!

Life with and for God is never walled in—confined to a room where one lives day after compartmented day. No, it is more like standing on a mountain with all the world before you, challenging you to explore the depths of the valleys and the heights of the hills.

Daily joy and victory are guaranteed by the risen Christ. Christ, the Victor, is true to His word and gives whatever we need to live this day in a spirit of praise. He makes our imperfect works of time count for eternity. Christ has accomplished His purpose; nothing can thwart His program. Christ rules the world; His power cannot be threatened. Life with and for Him is triumphant!

Throw yourself into such life today! And "go from strength to strength" (Ps. 84:7a).

60. HALLELUJAH!

"Praise him with trumpet . . . with lute and harp!
Praise him with timbrel . . . with strings and pipe!
Praise him with loud crashing cymbals!
Let everything that breathes praise the Lord!
Praise the Lord!"

Ps. 150:3-6 (RSV)

The stage is set for a festival of praise. The instrumentalists are in their chairs—no empty places. The orchestra is complete—brasses, strings, woodwinds, percussions, and all the special instruments, such as the timbrel (tambourine), for accent. The keynote is sounded so that all may be in tune.

Then the chorus enters—different faces and colors but all dressed alike and all radiating joy. What a procession! What grandeur! What numbers! And again there are no empty chairs.

The leader enters, and we expect the performance to begin. But, no, this is different. This occasion is not a performance. This is a festival! There are no spectators; there are only participants. The leader gives the cue, the trumpet sounds, and with perfect timing and harmony, all begin to play and to sing the same song. No one needs any music, for the theme is familiar: "Praise the Lord! Praise him for his mighty deeds!"

The music rolls out. Praise bursts forth. It fills the sanctuary; it resounds through the whole earth and beyond (v. 1).

There is excitement and exhilaration but no exhaustion. The works of the Lord provide lasting substance for song, and the Spirit of the Lord gives the breath for endless praise. Endless praise! The works of redemption took place in time, but the celebration of them cannot be limited by time.

Practice singing the songs of heaven today so that you may join heaven's choir, singing:

"Hallelujah!
Salvation and glory and power
belong to our God . . ."
Rev. 19:1a (RSV)